formatio

TRADITION. EXPERIENCE.
TRANSFORMATION.

Formatio books from InterVarsity Press follow the rich tradition of the church in the journey of spiritual formation. These books are not merely about being informed, but about being transformed by Christ and conformed to his image. Formatio stands in InterVarsity Press's evangelical publishing tradition by integrating God's Word with spiritual practice and by prompting readers to move from inward change to outward witness. InterVarsity Press uses the chambered nautilus for Formatio, a symbol of spiritual formation because of its continual spiral journey outward as it moves from its center. We believe that each of us is made with a deep desire to be in God's presence. Formatio books help us to fulfill our deepest desires and to become our true selves in light of God's grace.

SOULCARE® RESOURCES

Spiritual Formation for Individuals and Groups

SIMPLICITY

MINDY CALIGUIRE

IVP Connect

An imprint of InterVarsity Press
Downers Grove, Illinois

InterVarsity Press
P.O. Box 1400, Downers Grove, IL 60515-1426
World Wide Web: www.ivpress.com
E-mail: email@ivpress.com

InterVarsity Press® is the book-publishing division of InterVarsity Christian Fellowship/USA®, a student movement active on campus at hundreds of universities, colleges and schools of nursing in the United States of America, and a member movement of the International Fellowship of Evangelical Students. For information about local and regional activities, write Public Relations Dept., InterVarsity Christian Fellowship/USA, 6400 Schroeder Rd., P.O. Box 7895, Madison, WI 53707-7895, or visit the IVCF website at <www.intervarsity.org>.

All Scripture quotations, unless otherwise indicated, are taken from the Holy Bible, Today's New International Version™ *Copyright © 2001 by International Bible Society. All rights reserved.*

Design: Cindy Kiple
Images: chair: Iain McKell/Getty Images
*   room interior—2 chairs: Philip and Karen Smith/Getty Images*

ISBN 978-0-8308-3522-5

Printed in the United States of America ∞

P 20 19 18 17 16 15 14 13 12 11 10 9 8 7 6 5 4 3 2

Y 24 23 22 21 20 19 18 17 16 15 14 13 12 11 10 09

CONTENTS

My Heart Gods Home

INTRODUCTION
Confessions of a Closet

When I first began learning about simplicity I decided to tackle a closet in our home that I called the black hole. The process, I thought, would be fairly straightforward. Empty the entire closet, face whatever was there, and ruthlessly, even prayerfully, discern if each item really belonged there. I began with a lot of energy, optimism and ambition.

Here is just some of what I found: six years of family photographs, a half-finished cross-stitch project that hadn't been touched since 1988 (cross-stitch is a type of needlework that nice Christian women did in the eighties), Christmas gifts I had purchased for family members at a summer sale two years earlier, and four years' worth of baby clothes waiting to be ironed (whoever invented baby clothes that require ironing must have been seriously deluded or heavily staffed). The finest moment came when my son Jeffrey, then seven years old, saw the ironing board and asked, "Hey Mom, what's that?" He had never seen one.

Whatever you think of my housekeeping skills, this was a closet full of duplicity. It was loaded with false versions of me. Some versions were not real for that season of life; some were never real. While I had to fight off that shaming voice as I discarded and donated, I also felt the swelling of freedom and lightness. A deep sense that maybe, just maybe, it was okay to be who I was. That living within the boundaries of who I am is exactly what following God should look like. To cling to anything else means running my race heavily encumbered. Not everything that slows us down is sin, but if it slows us down from living the life we were designed to live, then it needs to be thrown off just the same.

My husband made the mistake of walking through my simplicity project and asked, "Mindy, I thought you were going to clean the closet?" It did look much better when the mess was hidden behind the closet door. We both laughed, and I reminded him—and myself—that this kind of work means things will get worse before they get better.

If you are willing to take a step toward simplicity, you're in for a similar process. Sure, take on a garage, drawer or other black hole for starters, but the real work of simplicity lies when you open the doors of your interior world and start pulling everything out and holding it up to God's discernment and love. You must ask yourself and God what stays, what goes and what, if anything, needs to be added. It may require enlisting the help of a spiritual director or close friend. The goal is to honestly and courageously determine what is in your life as a result of duplicity—living through a false self—and what is authentic.

The Path of Soul Care
Soul Care Resources are designed to offer a simple, but not simplistic, path for maintaining or recovering the life and health of your soul— that essential personhood created by God as *you*.

This book is divided into four experiences. Within each experience are four distinct parts that could be used as daily readings. Some parts are longer than others, so feel free to take more than a day to cover the material. Each part builds on the other, so you'll want to read one part at a time and reflect on the questions embedded in the text.

If daily readings aren't workable for you, just spending a day or two with each of the parts should allow you to comfortably complete one experience in a week, and the entire guide within about a month.

The fifth section of each part includes a discussion starter that you can use with a small group or friend if you wish.

I hope as you engage the path toward simplicity, you too will feel a swelling in your soul of freedom and lightness. A deep sense that maybe, just maybe, it's okay to be who you are. I hope you'll come to discover that living within your true self's identity is exactly what allows you to follow God completely, wholly. And, I hope that you will sense the wind in your hair, blowing across your face, as you run with great joy and intensity the unique race marked out by God just for you. Godspeed!

"Everything should be made
as simple as possible, but not
simpler."

ALBERT EINSTEIN

EXPERIENCE ONE / *Seeking Simplicity*

1 DID YOU WANT AN EASY LIFE?

The tag line of *Real Simple* magazine is "Life Made Easier." No wonder it's one of the top forty best-selling magazines in the United States! Goodness knows, we often feel the need for an easier life.

Maybe the *Real Simple* people are behind the "easy button" available at Staples office supply stores. A friend of mine actually has one that he keeps on his desk. Whenever things at the office get hard, he presses the large red push-button, which then loudly proclaims, "That was easy!" Maybe you can think of one or two projects that could use an easy button right now. Even if it doesn't accomplish anything, it might make you feel better to push the button!

As we embark on a journey toward simplicity, is that what we most need? For life to get easier? Is that how life becomes better and more vibrant? According to Staples and *Real Simple,* perhaps. And the appeal is certainly there.

■ What contributes to the stress level in your life these days?

The complexity of my relationships, my disorganized pantry and garage, my work commitments, and the overall complexity of life these days all seem to stand in direct opposition to a more manageable, easier life. Now, to be fair, I have read my share of *Real Simple,* exorcised (and sometimes accessorized) the unnecessary junk from my share of closets and experienced the joys of decorating with white. But I have also discovered that there is a deeper and truer path to simplicity that stems from a far more interior place—a place deep within my own soul. This place is not cluttered with dusty Christmas gifts or wrinkled laundry; it's cluttered with false versions of myself.

The interior path of simplicity is one I must walk if I want to live out my days in deep alignment with the person God has created me to be. I need to get rid of the false versions of myself that are cluttering my soul, because I've learned that, from a spiritual perspective, the enemy of simplicity is not complexity at all, but rather duplicity.

If you're like me, the very mention of the word *duplicity* makes you more than a little bit uncomfortable. It's not exactly on the "mostly okay" list of vices! *Duplicity* is used to describe double-dealing, two-faced, sneaking-on-your-taxes kinds of people. Surely not *I!* But we'll explore together how the temptation toward duplicity can and often does cause us—all of us—to live from various false versions of our true self. Sometimes we may be aware of this process, but often we're not.

The path toward biblical simplicity calls us, instead, to a single-minded pursuit of God from which everything else flows. This interior simplicity yields great personal integrity and a deep alignment between who we are, who God is and, thus, how we live. We are focused on what matters. Experiencing freedom regardless of the complexity and degree of difficulty in our lives. It starts with facing duplicity.

■ How do you respond to the prospect of finding duplicity lurking in your soul?

The current stress level in your life, and now the wondering about duplicity, could threaten your sense of well-being and hope. I want to remind you of God's heart toward us. In the Bible God conveys great sympathy for the tremendous burdens we often bear. They are by no means a phenomenon of modern-day life. Jesus understood these burdens, experienced his own burdens and spoke to his followers, both ancient and future, about entering into a new way of life:

> *Take my yoke upon you and learn from me, for I am gentle and humble in heart, and you will find rest for your souls. For my yoke is easy and my burden is light. (Matthew 11:29-30)*

Is he offering us an easy button? Not exactly, but not that far from it either. He is offering a different way to live—a way that is readily available, though few seem to experience it.

Read Jesus' words again from *The Message,* a popular Bible paraphrase written by Eugene Peterson:

> *Are you tired? Worn out? Burned out on religion? Come to me.*
> *Get away with me and you'll recover your life. I'll show you how*
> *to take a real rest. Walk with me and work with me—watch how*
> *I do it. Learn the unforced rhythms of grace. I won't lay anything*
> *heavy or ill-fitting on you. Keep company with me and you'll*
> *learn to live freely and lightly.* (*Matthew 11:28-30* The Message)

■ What in this passage especially speaks to you right now?

■ What do you find challenging or hard to believe/understand?

■ What area of your life most feels like a burden these days? Use some
of the remaining space on this page to talk honestly to God about that
particular challenge. What do you most wish for? What feels particularly forced or ill-fitting?

2 PURSUING SINGLE-MINDEDNESS

Many ancient and modern writers on the spiritual life have pointed to the need to pursue a singularity of focus in following God. The New Testament writings of James, specifically, warn us of the precarious instability that emerges from being double-minded.

Dietrich Bonhoeffer wrote an entire chapter called "The Simplicity of the Carefree Life" in *The Cost of Discipleship*. Doesn't a carefree life sound like a good idea? Bonhoeffer writes, "The singleness of eye and heart . . . knows nothing but the call and word of Christ" (p. 119). For him, simplicity meant a singular, unwavering focus on Christ from which every other priority, relationship and decision would flow. And for him, that singularity meant standing against the rise of the Nazi regime, and ultimately led to his execution. And yet he experienced his life as one that was "carefree."

The phrase "singleness of heart" Bonhoeffer uses stems from the first translation of the Bible into English, the King James Bible. What does it mean? The King James translation of Colossians 3:22 reads, "Servants, obey in all things your masters according to the flesh; not with eyeservice, as menpleasers; but in singleness of heart, fearing God." Singleness of heart, then, refers to a purity of intention, or singularity of focus. A full or complete devotion.

The "singleness of eye" Bonhoeffer refers to is not used much in our day (beyond gargoyles and Cyclops), but the classic text from which this phrase emerges comes from Jesus' teaching in the Sermon on the Mount, his "how to really live" treatise: "For where your treasure is, there will your heart be also. The light of the body is the eye: if therefore thine eye be single, thy whole body shall be full of light" (Matthew 6:21-22 KJV).

Scottish theologian Thomas Chalmers challenged his nineteenth-century listeners to understand this connection between singleness of eye and heart. "It is because the eye most looks to what the heart most likes that singleness of eye is made to denote singleness of a heart, set up on heaven and its treasures" (*Sermons and Discourses,* p. 146).

The passage from the Sermon on the Mount provides one of the clearest commands given us in the Bible. Here Jesus offers true guidance in response to the specific stressors he knew we would experience.

■ Read Matthew 6:19-32. What connections would you make in your own life between the treasures on earth and the stuff that brings anxiety?

Stuff requires your attention, acquiring it, taking care of it, guarding it. This takes up your time and attention. Not being able to aquire it, or losing it will cause anxiety

■ Think of how timeless and yet how timely these potential worries are. Write about the last time you worried (or began to worry) about one of them. *I am guilty - My kitchen is still not finished some 5-7 years later. My husband is not a good provider. I have let Kym use the truck so I no longer have transportation at my disposal. I panic and have anxiety over paying the tuition*

16

Now read Matthew 6:33-34. *But seek first his kingdom and his righteousness and all these things will be given to you as well.*

fear.

Singular Focus

Learning to seek God and his kingdom first—choosing that as the singular focus of our life—may require a shift in our perception of the "simple" life. The life that unfolds for God's people who possess such a singleness of eye or purity of heart and purpose is rarely simple by the standards of today's culture. Often, there's no easy button in sight! *AMEN*

The Bible portrays many examples of those who, while pursuing a life of deep devotion to God, had very complex lives. Let's just run through a few examples.

- Abram was called by God "to go to a land I will show you." Right. Can you imagine the conversations at the rest-stops between Sarai and Abram? "Where are we headed, dear?" "Not sure, darling, but we'll know when we get there." The complexity factor in Abram's life dramatically increased as he followed his calling.

- Moses was undeniably called by God to leave a private, stable life, return to the land of Hebrew slavery and ask Pharaoh to release all the slaves. He moved into a life of greater complexity.

- How about Esther? The undercover Hebrew beauty queen had to go public, revealing her true identity and risking her life by approaching the king uninvited in order to spare her people.

The list could go on and on: Noah, King David, the prophets Jeremiah and Hosea, and on into the New Testament. Two of the often underrated heroes exemplifying the inordinate amount of complexity taken on in the name of following God are Mary and Joseph—Jesus' mother and earthly father. Their assignment was to endure public disgrace with an out-of-wedlock pregnancy, travel across the country by foot/donkey when the pregnancy was at term, give birth in a less-than-ideal setting with no family or friends nearby, run for their lives to Egypt (upon an angel's instructions to Joseph in a dream), find a way to make a living incognito for two years, then leave everything again and travel back to start over in Nazareth. How many folks would sign up for that in a "how to do the first three years of marriage" course? *Not Many!*

- Can you think of someone—a friend, mentor, historical figure or person from Scripture—whose life became more complex as they followed God? What about their example is most compelling to you?

  Peter, he loved the LORD like I do, yet in a moment when he took his eyes away his faith failed and he would drown, if not for the love & patience of our LORD.

- What about their example is most challenging to you personally?

  I must keep my eyes on JESUS, never look away.

Hebrews 11 records the example of many "heroes of faith": those who courageously followed God's plans for their life—even in the most complex, confusing and downright dangerous situations. From the standpoint of complexity, or making life easier, their lives were not marked by simplicity at all. But they shared exactly the definition of simplicity that I aspire to: singularity of purpose. Full and complete devotion to one thing. In that regard, their lives were entirely simple. They were deeply marked by integrity, deeply aligned—at a soul level—with who God made them to be.

In him I am good - I want him to be pleased.

18

Knowingly or unknowingly, they obeyed Jesus' ultimate directive for living (specifically in response to our many anxious thoughts): "But seek first his [God's] kingdom and his righteousness" (Matthew 6:33).

Simplicity means taking action to align one's exterior world with one's interior values and commitment to God, the way so many before us in Scripture and throughout history have. While it may mean our life becomes more complex, the obvious fruit of simplicity is a reduction of clutter on many levels: materially, emotionally, in our schedules or in our closets. Through simplicity we become consistent and experience alignment, integrity, wholeness. We live out the values we profess; we discard what doesn't serve us. We feel complete—not pulled in many directions but rather resolutely pursuing the one path that really matters.

■ How does the new definition and picture of simplicity that's offered in this part strike you? *It it something I strive for - I have not balanced well in the past, and I totally bought into the American - You can have it all. That's really not possible - GOD created balance rest & work with my eye on Jesus I will preserve and work toward the balance.*

■ What about it, if anything, is appealing? What, if anything, makes you nervous? *The anxiety of the World's demands. On schedules, time tables, money due children to care for. For myself I am ready to sign on - How do I provide for Kate, Kym?*

■ Read 2 Corinthians 4:18: "So we fix our eyes not on what is seen, but on what is unseen, since what is seen is temporary, but what is unseen is eternal." How does this connect to our new understanding of simplicity? *The World is like a kaleidoscope of bright colors that hurt your eyes but draw your attention - Jesus is a pure light simple but pure where you can bask.*

Hebrews 12 provides very practical advice for pursuing God with singularity of purpose.

> *Therefore, since we are surrounded by such a great cloud of wit-*
> *nesses, let us throw off everything that hinders and the sin that*
> *so easily entangles. And let us run with perseverance the race*
> *marked out for us, fixing our eyes on Jesus, the pioneer and per-*
> *fecter of faith. For the joy set before him he endured the cross,*
> *scorning its shame, and sat down at the right hand of the throne*
> *of God. Consider him who endured such opposition from sinners,*
> *so that you will not grow weary and lose heart. (Hebrews 12:1-3)*

4/19 *for this morning this is how I feel*
2016 The men and women listed in Hebrews 11, and many others throughout Scripture, ran their races successfully. No two races were the same: David wasn't waiting for his burning-bush moment, Esther wasn't seeking to free her people by threatening various plagues, and Jeremiah, sadly, wasn't given the option to be vindicated in any meaningful way. He died misunderstood and maligned. These individuals didn't follow a common path to be obedient to God, but each ran to finish the race God marked out for them.

Now, as we each run our races—as we live our lives, in other words—we are surrounded by these invisible witnesses. We look at their examples to find encouragement and strength and wisdom. They remind us that it is possible . . . it matters . . . it's worth it. But we are not called to run their races, or anyone else's. They successfully ran the race marked out for them. And we are invited to do the same thing—run the unique race marked out for us. Their example can spur us on.

■ Write out the four directives we are given in Hebrews 12:1-3. What expression do they currently have in your life, if any?

① Throw off everything that hinders us and the sin that entangles us -
② Run the race that is marked for us
③ Fix our eyes on Jesus
④ Consider him who endured such opposition from sinners, so that you will not grow weary and lose heart -

■ Which one seems the most confusing or challenging to you today? Why?

① throw off everything that hinders you -
I would like to been from the responsibility of sending the kids to Valley - and I do not mind the sacrifice but I literally do not make enough money - Randy does not keep his word but I am suppose to honor my husband
② are you changing the road of the race? How can I stop worrying about this? This concerns not me but my children lives, education, friends? Please help me with answers to these questions.

21

■ How do these four directives connect to the concept of simplicity we're exploring?

It seems simple materially although you nudged me okay pushed I have scaled back. I don't even really want to shop except to repair & refurbish our house. The countertop has rot, I only have a subfloor - I need to work on the patio - I would love a picket fence around the yard

a cozy cottage feeling

Here's the rub: many of us are in this race, attempting to follow God as we live our lives. But we're often running, or attempting to run, in wrong directions, with the wrong focus, with the wrong equipment. No wonder we get stuck!

Sometimes we attempt to run a very safe, or even a very ambitious, race, but it's one that was marked out for someone else—not us. We struggle because we are not running our race. Sometimes we fix our eyes on ourselves or on something or someone else, and we lose the power of our connection with Jesus as we run. And sometimes, we burden ourselves with unnecessary or even destructive add-ons.

These become significant barriers to biblical simplicity. The remedy? Fix our eyes on Jesus, allowing God to direct our path. Throw off that which slows us down, which could be sin (harming others and ourselves), or anything that hinders us. And run with perseverance the race marked out for us. God must have known we would need this reminder—that a major temptation we face is to quit or to run someone else's race.

By my people pleasing skills

Those not-sin-but-still-hindering-us obstacles are often difficult to discern. They're not glaringly wrong. They just get in the way. And

Yes they are.

22

often, that's where duplicity creeps in and slows us down or derails us altogether. Think back to my closet: none of that was exactly sinful, but clutter in my life limits my ability to run the race—live the life—God has marked out for me. The closet silently condemned me every time I walked by it. Guilt. Shame. Wasted space. Wasted potential.

■ Pause and bring to mind one physical space in your life that doesn't reflect who you truly are. What is it? The garage? Desk? Basement? Junk drawer(s)? What needs to go? What ought to be in there, but isn't?

Top of linen closet needs going through — Randy needs to work on all the junk in big garage — clean out linen drawer

How might the duplicity represented in that physical space be hindering you, even remotely? What silent message does that space give you?

*Work on schedules —
Bring one thing in —
Remove one thing —
Don't clutter schedules —
Don't add to budget —
Still does not add up on the
ledger sheet. ? Physically I cant
work 2 jobs - My
body cant handle it.*

23

What does it mean to be duplicitous? The word *duplicate* gives us a clue. A duplicate is a representation or copy of an original. When the word is attributed to human behavior, it means acting in a way that is double. It means that a "real us" exists somewhere, but we present a duplicate or false self in our own stead.

We may recoil at the thought of *deliberate* duplicity, but destructive modes of subtle, culturally acceptable duplicity abound in everyday life. And the temptations toward this more insidious form of duplicity usually revolve around the need for more—more time, more energy, more money, more accomplishments, even more of us.

■ Write about a recent time when you felt the need for more of "something" in your life (it could have been more money, more attractiveness, more hair, more time, more influence, more vacation). What raised that desire for more of that specific thing? What difference did you think more of that thing would bring?.

More money - a relief to continue at VCS, to purchase a car, finish our house, buy our house from Peggy, Pay for future education for Kym & Nate, have a retirement fund - Send money to Cryptal - Pay for twins preschool - Give financial aide to church plants, VCS, Paramount Ave, SPCA, smile train, sponsor a child ~

In those moments like the one you just recorded, we are tempted to live duplicitously. Learning to recognize the symptoms is vital if we are going to avoid living through a false self. Here are a few questions I ask myself in those difficult moments to uncover the temptation toward duplicity in my soul:

Am I feeling overwhelmed by options? Deciding between thirty different pediatric fever medicines or dozens of investment strategies or ministry opportunities I could accept is stressful. Having so many options can be relentless and exhausting, sucking mental energy right out of me. The options themselves will probably always be there. But when I start to feel overwhelmed by options, I begin to look for duplicity.

■ Think of a recent time when you remember feeling overwhelmed. What circumstances surrounded that feeling? How did you respond? What connection, if any, might there be to the temptation of duplicity in that situation? *J am overwhelmed with our financial nightmare and the consequences it may bring to my children Nate, Kym and unfortunately has brought to my daughter Crystal. I have tried to keen the race accept the job for lesser money that J feel you called me to - J am bringing some money into the house, but J can't support our family on what J make or send the kids to UCS.*

Do I feel burdened by impossible demands? Yes Too many deadlines, too many phone calls to return, too many homework assignments to check on, too much shopping to do, too many brownies to work off on the treadmill—the list goes on and on. I'm not always realistic about the limits of my time or energy. As a result, the false Mindy, who does not want to disappoint, says yes to too many things. When I sense my-

self flailing around and drowning in the impossibility of my schedule
and commitments and tasks, I begin to look for duplicity.

■ How about you? When did you last feel the weight of the world when
you looked at your schedule and to-do list? How might duplicity tempt
you at those times?

*these are the areas that I have been
working on and I have been much
more realistic.
It is the area of the finances that I feel
duplicity and the relationship with Randy –*

Am I buying more than I can afford? Virtually everyone faces financial challenges of some sort, but sometimes we make it harder
than it needs to be by adding debt into the equation. Overspending
and excessive consumer debt reflect a deep level of duplicity, living as
though there is more money than the bank account actually contains.
The core solution is not only financial budgeting and restraint but that
crucial soul-level simplicity. *Pay cash. Shop at the
thrift stores for almost everything*

■ Does this one strike close to home? If it does, don't despair—perhaps
this study on simplicity will be the launching point for a new "day"
in your life in this area! So much shame and regret and fear can be
absolved as you walk a path of integrity and simplicity. Take a moment
to speak directly to God about this tender area of your life right here,
right now. *As I write LORD I see the duplicity
It is between Randy and myself –
His lack of honesr, self control and
integrity - my shame and fear of his
actions - as I try to walk in honor
self control and integrity.*

26

Did you sense God responding to you in any particular way? If so, be sure to record that here too.

[handwritten: Yes - My shamed fear of Randy's actions.]

Do I frequently desire to be more than I am? When I feel the pull to be more confident, more together, more successful, more spiritual, more hard-working, more capable or more organized than I really am, I am tempted by duplicity. Succumbing to that temptation causes everyone around me to suffer. I detest the thought of being duplicitous, but I've had to face the hard truth that this kind of duplicity is the root of many evils in my life. In fact, my life became unmanageable at a level far more important than the appearance of my closets.

■ As you consider the above areas, what current struggle might be related to a similar root of duplicity? Who else pays the price for this (coworkers, friends, your spouse, children)?

[handwritten: Our children FATHER through Jesus I ask you What do I do? Honor my husband? pray for answers - In him Robin]

Take a few moments to talk with God about that right now.

By now you may be thinking, *Great. Can opened, worms out. Now what?*

Together, we'll walk through a path from duplicity into increasing simplicity and freedom—one step at a time. And the first step is always facing the truth of where we are. Well done!

I love the words of God to his people through the prophet Isaiah. May these words encourage you as we move toward simplicity together:

Forget the former things;
do not dwell on the past.
See, I am doing a new thing!
Now it springs up; do you not perceive it?
I am making a way in the wilderness
and streams in the wasteland. (Isaiah 43:18-19)

■ Do you perceive a "new thing" God may be doing? What is it?

I don't know

Talk to God about this new thing that you desire in your life—the simplicity of the carefree life! It may well be that God has begun to plant and nurture that desire within you (before you even sensed it).

Father, I do want the simplicity of the carefree life - a balanced work schedule, the kids at VCS, a car, a home complete, answering to your call through people you send my way - Honoring my husband - Having a husband with honor & integrity

5 GROUP DISCUSSION

Summary

The ever-present, often ever-increasing stress levels in modern life can press us to wonder, isn't there a better way? A simpler way? Thankfully, there is. A path toward freedom and energy and creativity and joy. But for many of us, that path will not necessarily reduce the actual complexity of our lives. For Christ-followers, the concept of simplicity has far deeper roots and more far-reaching implications than merely the state of our schedules or storage units. Embarking on a journey toward simplicity requires developing a singularity of focus—a deep refusal of duplicity—that allows us to carefully follow the narrow way extended to those who would "deny themselves and take up their cross daily and follow [Jesus]" (Luke 9:23).

Opening

What inspired your interest in studying simplicity?

The complexity of my life in this world striving for the simplicity of God's world.

Discussion

1. What, if anything, did you sense God stirring in you through this first experience?

My prayer of living a life of balance - I do not have that lifestyle - To be honest my husband is a taker and I am a giver - He will take until I shut down. This is not a balanced life

2. What one or two ideas stand out? Why did they stand out to you?

Throw off everything that hinders - I guess I must do this every day sometimes twice a day - I Because I don't have the answers to my questions burden is light.

3. Read Matthew 11:28-30 out loud, and then return to your answers at the end of part one. Discuss your responses to the questions in this section. *Come to me all you who are weary and burdened, and I will give you rest. Take my yoke upon you and learn from me for I am gentle and humble in heart and you will find rest for your souls. For my yoke is easy and my burden is light.*

4. Describe someone who typifies a singularity of focus on God; it could be a historical figure, friend or family member.

Sister Teresa

5. Which symptoms of duplicity (part four) are you most likely to experience?

More Money

6. Read Isaiah 43:18-19. Describe to the group some of the "new things" you sense, or hope, God may be doing in your life right now. *Forget the former things, do not dwell on the past. See I am doing a new thing Now it springs up, do you not perceive it? I am making a way in the desert and streams in the wasteland.*

Prayer

If you feel comfortable, have one or several group members close this time in prayer.

Before the next gathering, everyone should complete "Experience Two: Dealing with Duplicity."

→ I hope he is preparing a way for the kids to stay at VCS.

"We are only falsehood, duplicity,
contradiction; we both conceal
and disguise ourselves from ourselves."

BLAISE PASCAL

EXPERIENCE TWO / *Dealing with Duplicity*

1 IT'S NOT ABOUT COMPLEXITY

I hope you're starting to feel two things: discomfort and hope. Discomfort from the prospect that duplicity may in fact lurk in your soul as it has in mine, and hope from the truth that there's another way to live, another way to run this race—one that won't suck the very life out of you!

How will this process work—the process of moving toward simplicity? As with any soul work, it begins with the sure hope that you too can experience the simplicity of the carefree life.

> *I have in mind something deeper than the simplification of our external programs, our absurdly crowded calendars of appointments through which so many pantingly and frantically gasp. These do become simplified in holy obedience, and the poise and peace we have been missing can really be found. But there is a deeper, an internal simplification of the whole of one's personality, stilled, tranquil, in childlike trust listening ever to Eternity's*

whisper, walking with a smile into the dark. (Thomas Kelly, A Testament of Devotion, *p. 45).*

Do you believe such a way of life could be possible for you? Stop a moment and let that question sink in. My life with Randy—

It is possible. The journey is not without difficulties, but the process will bring joy and freedom even as you face the obstacles. To aid you in your journey, we'll look together at one significant barrier to choosing simplicity, we'll pick up a few useful supports, and we'll examine some specific, classic sources of duplicity in everyday life.

A Big Barrier

One of the biggest obstacles in my journey toward simplicity was a deep—and unknown—fear about the truth. As I began my journey, one spiritual guide advised me, "Mindy, you've got to let what's going on in your head come out of your mouth." What strange advice! And how desperately I needed it.

Some folks don't have that problem; they've never had an unexpressed thought! But for me, the opposite was true. I was tightly wrapped in a straightjacket of "truth"—the truth of what I thought life was supposed to be. When real life didn't match up to that vision, I suppressed my experience, my thoughts, my opinions, my judgments, myself. Not everything going on in my head was good or right, but even when it was, I was terrified to talk about my views, hurts, thoughts, questions and anger. And I didn't realize I was afraid until I tried! Only then did I realize the crippling fear that had kept me quiet for so long, thinking I was doing the right thing.

I specifically recall trying to write about a fear I had in a journal. Midway through the sentence "I am so afraid that . . ." I literally

We are not wired in this way.

34

crossed off the words and instead wrote, "There is no fear in love. But perfect love drives out fear, because fear has to do with punishment. The one who fears is not made perfect in love" (1 John 4:18). I couldn't even be honest with myself about my fears, much less express them in healthy ways to others. The *truth* of God's promise never came to calm my actual fears; I just glossed over and further suppressed them. And my silence, as you might imagine, often led to duplicity. *Is this me?*

So for many months, I decided to stay with my friend's advice—to let what was going on in my head come out of my mouth (for the simple fact of integrity, if nothing else). Though I'd struggled to express my fears even in a journal, that's where my process really ended up starting. The safe, inviting pages of my journal became a nonjudgmental place to expose what was banging around in my head. I really wasn't ready to let much come "out of my mouth" at that point, but the safety of a journal offered a good place to practice. *I agree*

■ How about you? Do you tend to let what's going on in your head come out of your mouth, or are you more likely to stuff things down? Why?

Oh I am a stuffer -

■ Whether you are able to speak your thoughts or not, what are some of the "hard to accept" truths about your life right now?

That Randy doesn't listen to me - He only hears what he wants to hear. and I continue to try to see him in Jesus eyes and love him with agape love.

■ What fears might threaten to keep you silent?

Our family falling apart - this would be hard for the kids -

In light of this particular barrier, I'm suggesting you pick up some supports for your journey.

A journal. As you work toward building a life of true biblical simplicity, be sure to keep a journal in which you, too, can record your observations, discoveries, learnings and personal reflections. A journal's blank pages are a noncondemning, nonjudging, open invitation to express what is most true. In your pursuit of simplicity, the raw truth about life, about yourself and even about God will be essential. *OK*

■ How comfortable are you with recording your thoughts/feelings/ observations in the pages of a journal? Will this assignment be a stretch for you, or an easy one?

A Blank journal - tough - a thought provoking journal I can do and I am doing.

Start the process right now. As you consider embarking on a journey toward true simplicity, what are you looking forward to? What worries you, if anything? (Write it in your journal, not here!)

To highlight the start of something new, begin a fresh page in your journal (the first page if it's a new one) to describe a basic overview of your current season of life. How old are you? What is your family like? What do you do for work or school? What are the current stress points in your life? What's your current relationship with God like? Be as specific as you can.

A soul friend. In addition to a journal, I'd also suggest you recruit at least one soul friend to accompany you on the journey. Whether it's for a new exercise program, a new job or a new academic pursuit, the "buddy system" works. Why? The wise author of Ecclesiastes observed this phenomenon thousands of years ago. He wrote, "Two are better than one, / because they have a good return for their labor: / If they fall down, / they can help each other up. / But pity those who fall / and have no one to help them up!" (Ecclesiastes 4:9-10). *LORD, I need a buddy.*

In any journey, it's reasonable to assume a few things: we'll probably get lost or disoriented a few times. We'll probably fall down and may get hurt once or twice. We may run out of supplies or get slowed down by circumstances outside our control. In each of these cases, traveling with a soul friend can ease the load and ensure that we reach the destination. Plus, it's a lot more fun to share the experience with others!

■ Who might be some prospective traveling companions among your current relationships? *I have no idea - I do not have access to regular transportation, I don't see my old girlfriends or have time to talk with them like I use to.*

37

■ How could you go about asking for their support as you embark on a path toward simplicity?

LORD, I pray that you help me work on this area of my life.

I urge you to face the truth, whatever it is. Let whatever is true about you be known somewhere, and ideally to someone.

Keep in mind, the truth will set you free. Sound familiar? Jesus gave this radical insight to his followers in the Gospel of John, chapter 8. Often, in an attempt to be free, we actually hide the truth. Jesus offers us a better way, a truer way, a counterintuitive way. As another wise friend reminded me, "Truth does always set you free. No matter how hard that truth is, facing it will set you free."

Right now on our journey, you might be terrified of what we're going after. But as we take our next step—exploring classic temptations to duplicity—truth will alternatingly guide and propel us: guide us toward what is real, and propel us forward in our quest, perhaps even opening new options and new ways.

Live as free people, but do not use your freedom as a cover-up. (1 Peter 2:16)

LORD, my duplicity - still trying to people please. Help me to stop and please just you

Psalm 37

*You are the light of the world. A city on a hill cannot be hidden.
Neither do people light a lamp and put it under a bowl. Instead
they put it on its stand, and it gives light to everyone in the house.
In the same way, let your light shine before others, that they may
see your good deeds and glorify your Father in heaven. (Matthew
5:14-16)*

For me, the practical journey toward simplicity began with a source
of duplicity that became easy enough to see once I actually looked at
it: how I interacted with people far from God. While painful to admit,
I often did the very thing Jesus poked fun at: I put my light under a
bowl—even as a church-planter who aspires to reach out to those far
from God! Moving toward simplicity in this area of my life has been
both freeing and fun!

Do any nonbelievers know the real you? My Christian friends knew
I struggled with hope at times, argued with my husband, worried
about money and didn't like certain things about myself. My non-
Christian friends, however, only saw a Mindy who needed nothing.
In hindsight, I realized I was relentlessly cheerful and eager to share

various truths about my faith. I would have hated me. It took time for me to understand that every time I related inauthentically, I effectively put my light under a bushel.

Practicing simplicity in my words, especially with those far from God, means saying what's true, saying what's authentic. This has changed forever what it means for me to "share my faith." Now I stick to my real-time, here-and-now, in-the-moment experience of life with God. I am sharing my faith, not just a set of doctrinal statements (as important as they are).

■ What words best describe your relationships with those far from God?

EVERY DAY I PRAY FOR THE LORD's LIGHT TO SHINE FROM ME THROUGH THE HOLY SPIRIT- MY PROBLEMS ARE GREAT-MY MARRIAGE IS HARD- OUR FINANCES SMALL!

■ How might you inadvertently be covering the light in your life?

By Being a People Pleaser!

■ What, if anything, keeps you from speaking openly about your real-time faith (not just the doctrinal truths)?

I speak more of real-time faith than doctrinal truths for that is what keeps me going.

40

■ Take a minute to consider this past week and the interactions you've had at school, at home, at work, at the grocery store or in your neighborhood. When did you feel the pressure to "present" something, and when were you free just to be "present" with someone? What happened?

Two girls came in wearing T-shirts from their Children's ministry day — I told them I liked their T-shirts and conversation from many customers ensued with them —

Spend some time reflecting and praying about this right now. How would you like those experiences to be different in the future, if at all?

It was good from the context of being a

■ Make this a specific assignment before you move on in this study: Pay attention to any opportunity you have to meaningfully connect with someone far from God. See if you can focus on authenticity and a true expression of the life you have with God. In the space below, or in your journal, record your answers to these questions:

(employee.)

• What happened? *Two women, a mother & daughter very cranky (mean) I could not do anything right - Always felt like I was being slapped - I prayed & talked it over with the LORD - Do your best - don't take it personal - They do not have joy -*

• What feels different for you, and how did you sense God's presence with you in that encounter? *Next time I saw them I did the same - mother sharp, but soften, daughter came back to thank me - I called out have a blessed day -*

• What did you observe or learn through this experience?

Another customer came up and told me how she liked that - God's hand was all over it - He heard me - I was obedient - HE Blessed —

First Peter 3:15 says, "Always be prepared to give an answer to everyone who asks you to give the reason for the hope that you have." Peter assumes we will live among the lost in such a way that they can observe authentic hope. No one will be asking for the source of your false, plastic, forced hope. But do you have sincere hope in the face of emotional pain, hard relationships, financial setbacks or even physical illness? If so, would those family members and friends in your life who are far from God sense it? I suppose we'll know they can sense it when they start asking us.

Even as I write this today, I'm thinking through the past few months. While I have experienced profound hope and deep connection with God, it's been awhile since I've had a conversation like this with someone far from God. I wonder if, unknowingly, I've recently gotten back under that bowl. I want the hope I have to be authentic, visible, intriguing.

■ Use the following space to talk with God about your recent conversations with those he so deeply loves.

LORD, use me as you like - My only hope is in you. My marriage is difficult at best. My husband a selfish bully - I can only not feel wounded when I look at him with your eyes. My heart cries out for my children and saddness overwhelms me in not being able to provide for them. I am tired. I am weary. Forgive me. Thank you for your many blessings.

Are you living the life you were uniquely created for?

> *Body and soul contain thousands of possibilities out of which you can build many identities. But only in one of these will you find your true self that has been hidden in Christ from all eternity. . . . Identity is never simply a creation. It is always a discovery. True identity is always a gift of God. (David G. Benner,* The Gift of Being Yourself, *pp. 14, 16)*

The entire concept behind the word *calling* presumes that there is a caller. One who sees the bigger picture and invites us into a unique role in the grand scheme of things. "For we are God's handiwork *[poiema],* created in Christ Jesus to do good works, which God prepared in advance for us to do" (Ephesians 2:10). Our English word *vocation* has as its root *vocal* or *voc,* meaning "voice." A vocation, then, is a response to a call.

To pursue our calling or vocation, we need to acquire the ability to hear, to listen and to respond. One of the many sources of guidance in the process of understanding our calling is the way God has created us in the first place. God didn't create the horse to swim, or the eagle to burrow under the snow. Their very designs point to the purposes for which they were created, and the same holds true for us. Eagles and horses, however, are not tempted as we are. (Apparently, they don't look around the animal kingdom and wish for things they didn't get. But I do wonder about our cat sometimes. I think she's trying to be a sloth.)

Romans 12 urges us to willingly abandon our tendency toward self-gratification and instead embrace the call of God on our lives in transformation and service. And in that process, Romans 12:3 particularly challenges us to be sober-minded in our assessment of ourselves.

When we wrongly pursue avenues of work God never had in mind when he designed us, or when we refuse to use the gifts we have been given, we hurt both our families and churches. We must be sober-minded, making decisions based on who we *really* are, not on who we *want* to be.*

■ How has God crafted you uniquely? What are some of your strengths and talents and skills? In what ways does God seem to work through you in other people's lives? Once you have greater clarity on who it is God has made you to be, it becomes far easier to choose the path that will lead to simplicity. Write out your answers to some of those things here. *I'm not sure of these answers. He has called me to hospitality, to smile and care and bless. But not to people please. I must be careful not to cross the line. He seems to put me in peoples lives that may need some guidance, who may ~~what~~ wish to know the source of my light.*

*Two tremendous resources for me in understanding this were Parker Palmer's book *Let Your Life Speak* and Dan Allender's *To Be Told.*

I pray each day for his light to shine through me.

■ Which areas of your work/contribution seem to flow most naturally from who you are? Which roles are in conflict with your design? What do you observe about the difference between those two areas?

To care and bless - somehow for me cross over to people pleasing - My objective please GOD.

Sometimes our sense of who we are is buried so deeply within that it can be helpful to take a strengths assessment that helps pull the answers out of us.** The strengths assessment does just that and has been very useful to me in evaluating new opportunities; if they lay within my core strengths, I can consider the choice with greater confidence.

Remember, you are God's *poiema,* his workmanship, his unique piece of art, created with great value and purpose in his image. You were not created randomly, but with great specificity regarding the impact God intends for you to have in this world. When you live out of that true identity, it brings great peace and freedom into your life (as well as joy and fun and purpose and on and on).

Our purpose is not the kind of thing we can really screw up in any permanent way. Your design will always be with you—and if you're reading these words, you're still in a good place for God to bring to fruition that which he originally had in mind. It's never too late to start. If you're connecting meaningfully with God these days, you're on track.

**Strengths assessment developed by The Gallup Organization. The first edition is *Now, Discover Your Strengths* by Marcus Buckingham and Donald O. Clifton (New York: Free Press, 2001). The second edition is *The Clifton StrengthsFinder 2.0 Quickbook* by Tom Rath (New York: Gallup Press, 2007).

When you pursue the calling God has on your life, it may not decrease the complexity. Sorry, but that's just the case, and I don't want you to be caught off-guard if your life is still complex once you start pursuing simplicity.

Here is a story of simplicity: a simple life. Actually, two very simple lives: Kevin and Frank. My husband and I were both close friends with Kevin and Frank in college. They were part of the same fraternity, had come to faith in Jesus during similar times in college and were both star lacrosse players. By the time senior year came around, they were devoted Christ-followers actively leading in campus ministry. With characteristic intensity, they both sought God for direction once they graduated. Both considered moving into vocational ministry, but as they neared graduation, their plans changed. Radically.

Kevin left the halls of an Ivy League school and literally gave away every single thing he owned. In the spirit of St. Francis from long ago, he took up a life of intentional poverty among the poor and marginalized. Initially, he spent over three years living among and serving alcoholic homeless men in a Catholic center in upstate New York. Now, he and his wife, Emily, and their four children minister in one of New

York State's most impoverished areas: inner-city Syracuse. For many years, their home (in a nearby town) doubled as a L'Arche-related community home for a married couple with special needs. Kevin and Emily both serve as lay ministers within the inner-city parish of St. Lucy's. Theirs is a simple, very focused life involving little travel outside their community and relatively few possessions. As they expand the ministry to launch a nonprofit, offer more retreats and build collaborative relationships with other churches in their area, the focus remains tightly fixed to serving this location and these people. The complexity factor in a worldly sense is very low. But the simplicity is enormous. Kevin and Emily are living exactly as God has asked of them. And they find characteristic joy and peace in the midst as a result.

In contrast, Frank moved into his family's business in Baltimore and was soon named one of the top ten most influential business leaders in the city by local newspapers. At the same time (in his spare time!), he launched the first-ever Fellowship of Christian Athletes lacrosse team and established FCA in the Baltimore area, soon brimming with some three hundred high school students gathered in "huddles" in high schools across the area. He and his wife, Gayle, led a house church and were actively involved in their church and a crisis pregnancy center in Baltimore. His company grew 300 percent and became an active force for bettering the local community and a community far beyond the United States; through World Relief they adopted an entire village in Kenya and have faithfully been serving the needs of that community since the early 1990s. He played on the world lacrosse team for the U.S., and Gayle runs marathons. They have four active children, including two who have been adopted from Korea. Frank serves on the national board of FCA, remains very active in his church and continues to meet the challenges of a growing family business.

Frank's life is *very* externally complex. But it has a singularity of purpose to it—a deep integrity from which everything else flows. To know Frank is to know that he and Gayle (who teaches Community Bible Study for hundreds of women, and also launched and leads the national vision for teen-focused Community Bible Study) were *made* for this kind of living. They have been given substantial means by which to live very generous lives, and they do. Their many-faceted "doing" flows from a deeply centered "being." I love them for it! Their lives, just like Kevin's and Emily's, are a reflection of simple obedience to God, of surrendering decisions to God's guidance.

What I love about Kevin's and Frank's stories is that their relationship and friendship have remained despite the very different paths God has called each one to follow. Both Kevin and Frank are examples to me of biblical simplicity. Each is running the race marked out for them with terrific intensity and integrity, remaining faithful to the gifts and talents and passions placed there, for a purpose, by God. That's the kind of simplicity I want—one that obeys God wholeheartedly no matter what anyone else is doing.

■ What do you think of these two stories as examples of simplicity?

The heart of the matter - simplicity - Be obeident to GOD's WILL

■ What parts of your own story connect with the stories of Kevin and Frank? *I want to be obeident to GOD's WILL -*

5 GROUP DISCUSSION

Summary

Though we may cringe at the thought, we struggle with duplicity. It creeps into the most insidious places of our souls, negatively influencing many important areas of life, including how we relate to people we care about and, tragically, how we determine our life's work. Facing duplicity requires people who help us face truth and live in truth. The outward results vary, but the common, essential quality of a simple life, biblically speaking, is a resounding "Yes!" to God.

Opening

Have you ever felt cheated by false advertising on a product that appeared to have more than it actually did? A bag of chips or a bottle of hand lotion? Maybe a vacation destination? Tell a story from your own life.

Discussion

1. What, if anything, did you sense God stirring in you through this second experience?

2. Go back over your written responses to parts one through four. What one or two ideas stand out as something you'd like to bring

to the group? Why did they stand out to you?

3. Talk about your response to the first question in part one. Do you
   tend to express everything, or do you suppress it internally?

   I am by nature a stuffer. I have worked on this area - I regularly speak with the LORD.

4. Read Matthew 5:14-16. Who among your friends or family knows
   you really well and yet is far from God? How well do you let them
   see the "light"? *Many co workers - step children Scott & Jennifer - My sister, Randy's family I try to live my life by the light with the help of the Holy Spirit*

   Did you complete the assignment on page 41? Share with the group
   what happened. *Yes*

5. How congruent is your current area of work—whether it's in or
   outside of your home—with how you are "wired"?

   Except for being able to approach people with the word its very congruent -

6. Have there been times in your own life when whole-hearted obedience to God actually added complexity to your life rather than
   removed it? What happened? *Yes many times. I was in prayer much of the time - GOD's plan is always best!*

Prayer

Have one or several group members close this time in prayer.

Before the next gathering, everyone should complete "Experience
Three: Moving Toward Simplicity."

"The ordinary arts we practice
every day at home are of more
importance to the soul than their
simplicity might suggest."

                    THOMAS MORE

EXPERIENCE THREE / *Moving Toward Simplicity*

1 FACING THE LIMITS

In the first *Mission Impossible* movie, Tom Cruise descends into a vault and sprays dust into the air to expose a web of laser alarms. Once he's identified the boundaries, he's able to successfully navigate the passage.

Each of us has invisible limits, or "boundary lines," that provide a web of laser beams around the extent of our time, our intelligence, our willingness, our relational capacity, our energy and even our love. Invisible boundary violations destroy families, individuals, organizations and churches. Those violations show up as manipulation, shirking of responsibility and making commitments based on anything other than the truth of our limits.

Henry Cloud and John Townsend's landmark work *Boundaries* effectively sprayed the dust on those invisible laser beams around my life. That book revealed to me the boundaries that should have defined my own limits, but even though I had violated them—and allowed others to violate them—repeatedly, no alarms ever sounded when I crossed them.

■ When you consider limits to your energy, time, relational capacity or anything else, which ones do you tend to violate, if any?

In the past I violated all of them — I suppose if I am truthful, I still tend to violate these limits, but not all at once like before. I have trouble with my boundaries.

■ What circumstances or people are most apt to propel you into living beyond your limits? *My family - husband - Kids -*

■ What tends to happen under those circumstances?

After a period of time - I become overwhelmed and shut down - or explode

What place does duplicity seem to have in those experiences?

I try to buy into the woman bringing home the bacon - then cooking up the bacon - Doing it all like the media says

In 2 Corinthians 9:7 Paul says we should give what we decide in our hearts to give, *not reluctantly or under compulsion,* because God loves a cheerful giver. Though the context of this verse concerns financial

You can have it all !

54

giving to a community of faith, I've learned it applies equally to other things, invisible things, that I similarly can choose to give or not to give. During a season of overextension, I finally recognized that most of my "gives" had been reluctant or under compulsion. I felt I *had* to help, *had* to meet the need or *had* to solve the problem. Attempting to give what I didn't have crossed boundaries in my life.

Being a cheerful giver does not mean we should smile through gritted teeth as we give more than we have in our hearts to give. We certainly aren't called to give something we do not possess in order to gain God's approval. Instead, we need to live our lives "in the black" so we have something to give. Then we can freely, even cheerfully, write the check, make the phone call, join the committee or lead the team.

I so often opperate out of the Red

I've learned to think in terms of "clean gives." When an opportunity to give something of myself arises, it's time for some honest soul searching: *"Do I have it in my heart to give?"* If so, that's great! I give with no strings attached, freely, and I often do sense that God loves it.

But we may discover that sometimes the answer is no, we don't have it in our heart to give whatever is being asked. In that case, the path of simplicity would lead us to refrain. It wouldn't be a clean give. This is easy enough to write about, but very difficult to do! If you've been in the habit of responding to every request that comes your way, learning to say no to anything that takes you beyond the limits of your invisible boundaries will be a difficult task. But there's a lot of freedom on the other end!

At one point, I recognized that nearly all commitments outside my family had been made reluctantly or under compulsion. In a season of deep soul healing and restoration, I simply did not have much else to give. In order to honor the work of God in my life at that time, I

needed to gently set down every ball I had been dutifully juggling. It
was tormenting. But necessary.

■ Think through the current expenditures of your money, time, emotional energy and relational resources. Are they primarily clean gives?
Where do you sense you're giving reluctantly or under compulsion?

*My husband has a tendency to bully
me into getting his own way, whether
it is right or not. My Kids will
manipulate me. I have cleaned up
my act outside of the home.*

Facing Our Lack

You may find that you really don't have many clean gives going on
right now. Instead, you may find you are quite depleted and don't have
much of anything in your heart to give at all! For many of us that doesn't
sound very "Christian." What do you do? I faced that question head-on
when I began to walk a path of soul restoration and biblical simplicity.

Some people ascribe to the "fake it till you make it" philosophy
around spiritual matters like this. But I believe that is a dangerous path
to duplicity. Certainly there is a place for obedience even (or especially!)
when we don't feel like it. We continue to feed our children, show up
at work and pursue an authentic connection with God regardless of our
feelings. But even in these activities, if our heart is not really "in it," it's
important to talk with God honestly about that and explore with him
what really is going on in our heart. God meets us in our depletion.

Yes he does.

■ Use the space below to talk to God honestly about any areas of depletion, and ask for his guidance in future decisions.

*Father, please help me with Randy
Kym and Nate even Desi because
I am often so weary !*

The Committee of Selves

Quaker writer Thomas Kelly brilliantly describes how an overcrowded schedule, arising from duplicity, can actually start in our own head:

> *Each of us tends to be, not a single self, but a whole committee of selves. There is the civic self, the parental self, the financial self, the religious self, the society self, the professional self, the literary self. And each of our selves is in turn a rank individualist, not co-operative but shouting out his vote loudly for himself when the voting time comes. And all too commonly we follow the common American method of getting a quick decision among conflicting claims within us. It is as if we have a chairman of our committee of the many selves within us, who does not integrate the many into one but who merely counts the votes at each decision, and leaves disgruntled minorities. The claims of each self are still pressed. If we accept service on a committee in the community, we still regret we can't help with Sunday-School class. We are not integrated. We are distraught. We feel honestly the pull of many obligations and try to fulfill them all.*
>
> *And we are unhappy, uneasy, strained, oppressed, and fearful we shall be shallow. For over the margins of life comes a whisper, a faint call, a premonition of richer living which we know we are passing by.* (A Testament of Devotion)

■ Do you hear a faint call floating on the margin or your life? What is it? What premonition is coming to you of a different way of living? Talk directly to God about that right here.

FATHER, I WANT TO LIVE WITHIN MY MEANS — THIS ENTAILS FINANCIAL, SOCIAL, FAMILY — I WANT A BALANCE — AND I DON'T WANT TO ALWAYS FEEL LIKE I'm RUNNING TO CATCH UP —

Simplicity means a return to the posture of dependence. (*Richard Foster,* The Freedom of Simplicity)

How we actually live—not what may be written down on a personal mission statement or what we say in public settings—portrays our truest priorities. Our schedules and checkbooks reveal what is most important to us: what receives (and what doesn't receive) the majority of our time and energy.

The understanding that our exterior life is determined by our interior well-being should lead us into a different way of life: a way of life where we make feeding our soul a priority, where we abandon hurry and duplicity, where we seek the way that more closely resembles the yoke Jesus said would be easy and light. This is not a creedal call to ineptitude and laziness. Rather, it is a way of pursuing God as the source of our strength, releasing our illusions of self-sufficiency. We acknowledge who we really are and become comfortable with dependence. And it shows up in our schedule as time devoted to prayer, to solitude and even to rest.

■ What do you currently do to nourish that interior life with God?

I seek Bible study, prayer, journaling.

What priority do you give that soul nurture? Is the level of soul care sufficient to meet the demands of your current season of life? If not, what else do you imagine would help?

A service opportunity that would fit in my work schedule. Another Bible study group. (weekly)

■ Read Proverbs 4:23: "Above all else, guard your heart, / for it is the wellspring of life" (NIV). What might need to change in your life in order for you to experience this wellspring of life?

Enforcing my boundaries —

■ Quickly review your actual calendar from this past week (perhaps your checkbook too!). What do your actions (how you spent discretionary time and money) indicate the wellspring you pursued was? Was it connection with God? Something else?

*Education for Kids
Paying off debt   work
Doing for me - walking dog at beach
Repairing home   face products - rest.*

One important dimension to the care of our souls is our need for sabbath rest. Far from being restrictive or legalistic, the point of this intentional downtime is to offer up a portion of our time as an offering of sorts back to God. Resting in his care and love is a way of declaring our dependence upon him for everything. In the same way that fasting from food reminds us that God is the ultimate source of our life and strength, focusing our attention and worship back toward God and resting from our productivity and efficiency during a sabbath reminds us that God has created each of us for more than just work. And that it's really not all up to us.

In the Ten Commandments, God advised a full twenty-four-hour period of rest. But rarely do I have a schedule that allows for the same sabbath-rest day every weekend. (I have friends who do, and they love it!) Instead, I practice what I call a "twenty-four-hour floating sabbath," reserving a twenty-four-hour period each weekend during which I won't engage with what I feel makes me productive. It could be Friday night to Saturday night, or Sunday afternoon to Monday afternoon, or Saturday morning to Sunday morning (you get the idea?), but I take the entire twenty-four hours to rest with God and loved ones. Sometimes this choice is easy for me; at other times, it is a tenacious leap of faith as I set aside very pressing demands.

Simplicity asks that I live in the truth, however. And the truth is (1) I need rest, and (2) it is God who can be trusted for my future, not me. What's also true is this: I am not a slave to the law of sabbath-keeping. I am surrendering to this rhythm more and more as time goes by. Some weeks I really rest. Sometimes I am unable or, worse, unwilling. In all cases, I am learning.

For some kinds of "work" the choice to embrace a sabbath rest is more obvious than others, but both the invitation and the need are universal. So how about you?

■ What is restful, and even fun, for you?

*Going to the beach, walking the dog -
Watching a movie with the Kids -
Going thrift-shopping or yard saling -
Reading - Gardening*

■ What's the longest stretch you typically go without being "productive"?

*A couple of days - then the house
is a mess, things start stacking up and
I get antsy -*

■ What about your season of life or kind of work makes taking sabbath rest particularly challenging?

My work schedule

■ What, besides a demanding schedule, might be keeping you from giving yourself adequate sabbath rest?

My family -

If the idea of sabbath rest feels especially hard or impossibly unattainable for you these days, take the space below to talk with God honestly about that—and be sure to specifically ask for God's help. You never know what may open up: "You do not have because you do not ask God" (James 4:2).

*FATHER, Please help me
with Balance in my life.* 61

3 HONORING THE BODY

Or didn't you realize that your body is a sacred place, the place of the Holy Spirit? Don't you see that you can't live however you please, squandering what God paid such a high price for? The physical part of you is not some piece of property belonging to the spiritual part of you. God owns the whole works. So let people see God in and through your body. (*1 Corinthians 6:19-20* The Message)

Bathing, clothing, nourishing, having sex and even suffering all take place in relationship to the body. And far from being separate from the spiritual life, the body is central to the expression of our life with God. Dallas Willard writes, "For good or for evil, the body lies right at the center of the spiritual life" (*Renovation of the Heart,* p. 159). In fact, the core spiritual sacraments of baptism and Communion are inherently physical (whatever disagreements exist regarding their practice and place in congregational life).

Perhaps it's not surprising, then, that one of the sneakiest areas where duplicity lurks in our lives is in our physical well-being. And while much could be said regarding sexuality, suffering, clothes and cleanliness, we're just going to consider the need for simplicity in a few of the most obvious areas.

We know full well that our bodies require sleep, healthy nutrition and adequate exercise. And yet, despite the cultural obsession with thinness, perennial youth and physical beauty, public health statistics tell us our culture's actual health is in severe decline. We push ever onward through sedentary days and sleepless nights, consuming toxins and even otherwise healthy foods in deeply unhealthy ways.

What would simplicity look like in our physical self-care? Our bodies are not split apart from our souls; rather, we are "embodied" souls. The body is a physical dimension of our personhood and must be regarded and protected accordingly.

So let's start with sleep.

■ Do you know how much sleep your body needs in your current season of life? How much is it?

I need 8 hours -

■ Do you suspect you're not getting enough sleep? What are the symptoms? And if not, why are you not giving yourself the sleep you need?

Yes - after years of not getting enough sleep - I now know how important sleep is -

■ What would it take for you to stop living in sleep-denial and actually get the physical rest you need?

yes definitely have done this most of my life

We also need physical nourishment—food. This, especially, is a much larger topic. Do you tend to overeat? Undereat? Use food as a weapon or to medicate pain? Does it occupy more mental energy than it should? Do your eating patterns reflect a refusal to live within the "truth" of what you actually need? Yes, it's a big topic, one that involves our emotions and thoughts as well as our physical bodies.

In 2 Corinthians 10, Paul uses a particularly intense phrase to describe a way to protect ourselves from temptations or destructive forces. He urges his readers to "take captive every thought to make it obedient to Christ" (v. 5). Every thought? That's singularity of focus!

In practical terms, I understand this to mean that when a certain idea or thought or attitude becomes lodged in my brain, I have a choice. I can let it run its course, or gently grab it by the hand and lead it toward Christ where it can be assessed and then honored or dismissed accordingly.

When you have thoughts about food choices, particularly if this is an area of struggle, could you do the same? Bring them into obedience to Christ? I'm not sure God cares that much whether you have an organic apple or a Twinkie, but why not at least ask? Elsewhere, Paul urges us, "So whether you eat or drink or whatever you do, do it all for the glory of God" (1 Corinthians 10:31). Simple.

This evaluation may cause you to be more mindful of how much you actually consume. For others, this could cause you to consider the quality of what you consume (my ten-year-old son has begun checking for trans-fats on food labels!). For still others, this could mean paying attention to when you eat, responding to true hunger rather than external cues.

■ What's your relationship with food? What would a move toward simplicity look like for you in regard to food?

I eat when I am upset sometimes bored – But I find that when I'm busy and not falling apart I eat for substance. – I also like to eat gathered around the table – family time – friends etc –

Finally, let's talk about exercise. I trust you know the value and the importance of aerobic exercise, strength training and flexibility. If not, likely any health-oriented magazine or book can help you. But the question for us in this context is, how does your "practice" line up with what you know to be true? Are you giving your body what it needs? More focus than it needs?

■ Whether you struggle with too much or too little, why is that the case? What would it mean for you to live in line with truth there?

I struggle with time issues – I know it's not much, but if I could walk Meeka 30 minutes a day – It would be good – Jim standing all day now 5 days a week. Now I need to incorporate 30 min routine in my schedule – I need Balance in this area –

65

4 CONFRONTING THE CLUTTER

Most often when we think of simplicity, we expect to face the crowded closets, the ignored "basement part of the basement," the back wall of the garage, or even the top of our desk at work or school. So far, we have taken a different approach, looking at deeper, soul-level approaches to simplicity. Soul-level simplicity does correlate to our physical environment, though, as we have seen with the body. It's therefore time for us to take a quick look at the "stuff" of life—clutter.

As you pursue simplicity, you will increasingly become a better steward of the various spaces in your schedule, in your skin, in your home, in your car—in your life. The well-ordered heart extends to a well-ordered life, not because the neighbors are watching, but because the peace and well-being of your soul will extend gradually to everything over which you have been given responsibility.

Years ago, I read a typical magazine article on simplifying life. In it, the author presented a very interesting and spiritually significant observation about why we hang on to excess stuff, whether in the junk drawer, the closet, the cabinet under the sink or the attic. The reasons, he believed, all point to one thing—fear. Specifically, two fears.

Some clutter is kept out of a fear that we will be insufficient to meet the demands of the future. A variety of items in my own "black holes" came to mind. Who knows if I might need this one day? I've begun asking myself how hard it would be to retrieve the information or replace the item if I ever really did need it in the future, or (gasp) what would go wrong if I just didn't have that thing (sequined holiday belt/used baby onesies/sewing machine/article on clutter—okay, the article turned out to be helpful).

The other fear the author of the article observed was this: we hang on to clutter because we're afraid to face a regret from the past. It might seem small and trivial, but I suspect one of the reasons I never gave or threw away all my cross-stitch stuff is because I regret that I'm not the kind of woman who completes lovely handmade decorations and gifts. And because I don't want to face that regret, I just hang on to the unfinished business another year.

Do you see how the possible connection to fear has very spiritual implications for us? *I agree somewhat to the fear, maybe #1. #2 regrets are not why I might keep stuff — Memories could be #2 for me. -*

Extreme Simplicity Makeover

Try an exercise in joining together the spiritual process and a physical space. Begin by identifying a place in your house, in your garage, in your car or in any physical place that represents duplicity to you. Whether it's a closet that's overstocked with clothes you don't need or a junk drawer that you just haven't had the time to go through, identify that place. Then, set aside the time to do an extreme simplicity makeover. Professional organizers—closet exorcists—tell us the first step is to dump everything out (until you see the back wall). Then you clean the whole thing, and sort the contents according to what you will keep, toss, give away or recommission. Finally, you can put back only those things you will keep (and keep there).

This is not a do-it-yourself project, though. This is a do-it-with-God project. Start by dedicating this time to God. As you empty, clean, sort and re-store, speak with God about every single item (this may seem odd at first!). Learn the discipline and focus of asking, "How about this sweater? This extra can of paint from four years ago?" Pay attention to the resistance you feel, as well as any regrets, fears or other thoughts that may arise. Does God bring to mind a needy family who could use that sweater? Talk with him honestly about whatever comes up for you.

You could think of this as creating at least one corner of your physical world that is an expression of inner integration—it honestly represents who you are and what God is doing in you in this season of life.

■ Use the following space to record what project you did and what you learned through the experience. Specifically, how did you see duplicity reflected in the clutter, if at all? To be honest - I have been doing this - As have Randy - some stuff in the garage are antiques and furniture is not selling right now - For the house I have the top shelf of the hall closet and the top shelf of my closet -

■ How about fear? Again, what did you learn about yourself? What, if anything, did you sense God saying to you?
I learned that some stuff has memories attached - So sort the memories. Some stuff has value, but the market is down on furniture, but we are ready to let go -
68 My stuff with memories attached is the hardest to let go -

5 GROUP DISCUSSION

Summary

Often duplicity lurks in seemingly benign or even noble areas such as our commitments to others. But these murky waters of personal boundaries must be entered if we wish to run our race unencumbered. Moving toward a simple single-minded life requires facing the occasional disconnect between what we know and how we live, how we treat or mistreat our bodies. Even our physical space can become cluttered as a result of the internal lack of clarity. True freedom and lightness are available through a more integrated life.

Opening

What is one physical space that represents a bit of chaos in your life lately? The car? Garage? Junk drawer? Make-up stash?
The top shelf of the hall closet.

Discussion

1. What, if anything, did you sense God stirring in you through this third experience? *Balance: exercise, food choices, and eating habits into my schedule. Tackle the balance of stuff that needs to be sorted — Remember the rule —*

2. Go back over your written responses to parts one through four. *Bring one thing — Remove something —*

What one or two ideas stand out as something you'd like to bring to the group? Why did they stand out to you?

Enforcing my boundaries — Finding balance.

3. Return to your answers to the first three questions in part one. Talk about your responses to those questions.

4. Read 2 Corinthians 9:7. What's an example of a clean give that you've made since reading about this idea? *Giving is not my problem, finding a balance in giving and taking care of myself, so that I do not shutdown, is my challenge.*

   What's a pending decision that could be aided by asking, "Do I have it in my heart to give?" *My question- I have it in my heart to give, but how do I do it? I want to, give all, how do I find the Balance in this?*

5. What form, if any, does sabbath rest take in your life right now? What difference do you sense it makes in your ability to connect with God and in your ability to live a "simple" life? *I need rest weekly, I need time to worship and praise and to be with him. My focus on him - Keeps my*

6. Discuss what your Extreme Simplicity Makeover project was, and what you discovered as you accomplished it. What do you think the next project will be? *Balance of exercise, nutrition, rest. Balance of family.*

every focus clear. If I look I tend to become inundated with world things

Prayer

Have one or several group members close this time in prayer.

Before the next gathering, everyone should complete "Experience Four: Simplicity as a Way of Life."

"What am I supposed to do with my life?
The question of how to live our lives
especially presses on those of us who
sense we are not merely humans
trying to be spiritual, but are deeply
spiritual beings endeavoring to live
as fully human."

BRENT BILL, *THE SACRED COMPASS*

EXPERIENCE FOUR / *Simplicity as a Way of Life*

1 RIGOROUS HONESTY AND RUTHLESS TRUST

A major service of spiritual disciplines . . . is to cause the duplic-
ity and malice that is buried in our will and character to surface
and be dealt with. Those disciplines make room for the Word and
the Spirit to work in us, and they permit destructive feelings . . .
to be perceived and dealt with for what they are: our will and not
God's will. (Dallas Willard, Renovation of the Heart)

To grow consistently in simplicity we need to firmly establish two major qualities in our lives: rigorous honesty and ruthless trust. But how
do we become rigorously honest and ruthlessly trusting? Through the
help of spiritual disciplines.

The first quality, rigorous honesty, involves a willingness to face
those duplicitous parts of ourselves and see them for what they are:
false. We choose to abandon pretense and face the person in the mir-
ror with eyes wide open.

So far we've used journaling and reflection questions to help us recognize our false self. But there are other spiritual practices—three in particular that we'll look at here—that are useful in revealing both our duplicity and God's truth.

First, we discover truth about ourselves as we *study the Scriptures.*

For the word of God is alive and active. Sharper than any double-edged sword, it penetrates even to dividing soul and spirit, joints and marrow; it judges the thoughts and attitudes of the heart. (Hebrews 4:12)

■ Reflect on a time when you realized a truth about yourself as a result of time spent reading the Bible. What did you learn? What difference did that realization make, if any? Use the space below to write your observations. Doing the Breaking Free study — I realized how GOD had called me, and how He had been next to me, watched over me and protected me - Even when I did not know him.

We also encounter truth as we *connect with God personally in prayer.*

He [God] will give you another advocate to help you and be with you forever—the Spirit of truth. (John 14:16-17)

■ How about a truth you discovered through connection with the Holy Spirit? Perhaps it was conviction of wrongdoing, an awareness of an attitude, or desire or even a leading to make a particular decision regarding vocation. Write about a time when you sensed God's Spirit guiding you into truth about yourself. He guided me to the challenge of Dare to Love, and He redefined how I needed to love my husband. I do not resent or think of him as a mill stone around my neck. I now know the Blessings that God placed in my life.

74

Third, through intentional times of *soul searching,* we take an honest look inside, guided by the Holy Spirit.

Search me, God, and know my heart. (Psalm 139:23)

■ Have you ever sensed God answering a prayer like this for you? When? What happened? *I'm not sure which study - Maybe Psalms, but I have put my fear aside and prayed this prayer - I hate it when he shows me something else, but I know he does to grow me. He takes the time because he loves me -*

A second important quality we need to grow in simplicity is ruthless trust. It, too, is cultivated through intentional soul care. Journaling helps us see the choices before us and choose faith. Spiritual friends remind us of God's faithfulness over the years and encourage us to stay the course. Solitude strips us of the reinforcement we get from others—the external validation of our identity. Times of intentional soul searching invite God's Spirit to specifically guide our reflection process and lead us to transformation. Serving others in secrecy starves our tendency toward narcissism and creates space for authenticity and truth. Even just spending time in nature can expand our faith. Over time, as our trust in God and his ways grows, we can more easily walk the path of simplicity. When confronted by a temptation toward duplicity, we recognize it sooner for what it is and more gladly choose in favor of simplicity—no matter what the cost.

■ Of these two, rigorous honesty and ruthless trust, which comes more naturally to you? *Ruthless trust - I didn't have a choice. I have trust in the LORD, His will not mine. (I do give suggestions still) I can't do any of it on my own - I need his Holy Spirit - for I am a weak person.*

■ When you think of spiritual practices that help develop these qualities, which seem appealing to you?

Retreats - Bible studies -
I still am not entralled with the
knock you on your butt - Solitude thing
he has done in the past.

Simplicity as a way of life is a vision we pursue with great intensity—not from a shrill or rigid place of striving or fear, but because we long for freedom and life. We want to breathe deeply, sleep well and spend ourselves for causes with wisdom and great energy. Thomas Kelly ends his compelling chapter called "The Simplification of Life" thus:

> *Life from the Center is a life of unhurried peace and power. It is simple. It is serene. It is amazing. It is triumphant. It is radiant. It takes no time, but it occupies all our time. And it makes our life programs new and overcoming. We need not get frantic. He is at the helm. And when our little day is done we lie down quietly in peace, for all is well.* (Testament of Devotion, *p. 100*)

For those recovering from addictions, help can be found in twelve-step programs. But it's possible to sit on the sidelines of the twelve steps, observing but never experiencing the changes available. To really experience recovery, people often need to walk a more deliberate path through joining a step group. In these smaller, committed groups, people do far more than attend and listen. Each week, and between their weekly meetings, they "work the steps." The nickname for some step groups captured my imagination. They're called "AWOL groups," for those who are pursuing "A Way Of Life."

What a model for Christ-followers! A group of fellow journeyers, dependent on God, committing together to intentionally help one another grow by moving beyond passive acknowledgment of ideas—beyond attending and listening. We want to be disciples, not spectators. We want to be Christ-followers who intentionally pursue relationships, practices and experiences that, woven together, form a way of life. A new way of life that opens us up to the transformation that is available to each of us through a deepening, real-time relationship with God. A new way of life that calls us out, forward, into our God-given destinies.

This is what I want.

I always liked this vision of an AWOL group—an intentional gathering of those who were serious about the spiritual journey and the new way of life it leads to. The group would not be an elite clan for moral achievement or superiority, but just the opposite. We would gather in shared desperation and deep need, knowing that God is truly the source of our lives, both now and forever.

For me, going AWOL has come to represent two things in my spiritual journey. First, it means I am intentionally pursuing A Way Of Life, weaving together my experience of various spiritual practices so that I can remain attuned and responsive to the activity of God in my life. I am not after moral achievement or a self-congratulatory disciplined regimen. I am after life. I want to live—to live in the freedom and life God has made available to me and to each one of us.

But going AWOL also conveys that I am absenting myself from my former allegiance to the systems and power struggles and priorities of this world. Absent Without Leave. I am choosing another way (aspiring to it, anyway)—the way of simplicity, the way of life, the way of Jesus. I am no longer toying with the spiritual life. I have no more illusions: God is my life (see Deuteronomy 30:20). I fear this may sound too radical or brazen or bold or even pretentious, but I see it as my deep refusal to go with the flow, however imperfectly implemented.

I love the edginess of going AWOL in this spiritual sense. I am assigning, or reassigning, my allegiance singularly to the kingdom of God. Keep in mind that this is my ideal, my desire, a vision. When I forget, when I ignore God's whisper, when I move away from God's presence—and I most certainly do—there is still more grace. No condemnation, no hand-wringing, no self-recrimination. I pick up where

I left off. And you can too. It's about walking a path, not achieving anything.

You may wonder, is it hard to live this way? It takes everything and nothing. It's everywhere and nowhere. As Thomas Kelly said, "It takes no time, but it occupies all our time."

In the Company of Friends

I've found I need the company of a few close friends to help me walk away from duplicity and toward simplicity, so for some time now I have met weekly with my "simplicity group." I think of it also as an AWOL group—a place to intentionally seek growth by pursuing a way of life together.

Our aim is to help one another lead lives of full devotion—full surrender—to God, and to do that we've developed a very unusual format compared to other small groups I've been in. Everyone in the group is already familiar with core spiritual practices such as spiritual friendship, forms of prayer, solitude, silence, confession, serving, worship, fasting, sabbath rest, the use of Scripture (study, meditation and memorization), soul searching and journaling. Each participant has a special "simplicity journal" in which to record their observations and experience. We gather together for about two hours to work through a process much like the one outlined below.

1. First, we *share a meal together* (we bring our own lunch) and catch up a bit relationally.

2. Then, we *spend ten to twenty minutes in group solitude* (and "group solitude" is not an oxymoron!). We begin with silent prayer, then respond to some reflective questions.

(We don't all answer every question; just whichever ones seem most important that week.)

- Where did duplicity creep in for you this past week? How did you respond when you noticed it?

- How did your "practice" go this week? What did you agree to do, and what happened? (Each group member agrees to follow an intentional practice for the week. This practice could be a rhythm of prayer, study or fasting, or it could be an act of service, a commitment to rest, a time of solitude or silence, or invisible giving. We often find that God speaks to us through these practices.)

- Through what (Bible, other book, sermon, song, conversation) did you feel challenged or encouraged by God this past week, if at all? What did you sense God communicating to you?

- What "cramped choices" did you find yourself making? (This is a time for confession and being known in our sin.)

- Did any particular dream or desire for your life emerge this week?

3. Next, we each *talk about our solitude reflections* and discuss what practice we will pursue during the next week.

4. Finally, we *pray for one another,* both in ending the group meeting and during the week on our own.

■ Take the following space to reflect on each of these questions in your own life, and consider a practice that you could commit to for the upcoming week.

① Listening to a lonely lady — that turned to gossip — I shut it down, thought out a plan to use if it happens again. Shared it.

② I have not been consistent every day with journaling. It does seem that sometimes it takes me longer to digest some things.

③ This book, and a Circle of Quiet. He wants me to find a balance in my life, a rythm, a non destructive pattern.

④ Cramped choices. hurt feelings on Mother's Day Morning — worry and plan of action over Crystal, Kimberly & Nathan and following through

⑤ It is not a new dream — I dream for an end to financial hardship — To be able to pay tuition, help Crystal, purchase a car, repair & refurbish our home, ERC Purchase our home from Peggy — Give financial support to VFS, and many other non-profit groups anonymously,

■ Who could you share your desire to grow in simplicity with? What kind of format might serve you best?

Vickie Gelberg? My children? Co-Worker or Customer

Randy?

I'm not sure of the format — LORD will you help me with both parts to this question —

3 INVISIBLE SOURCE OF LIFE

The good news (the gospel) that Jesus conveyed to his listeners was simple: the kingdom of God is now accessible, through himself. It is, as he said, at hand. The stories he told and the way he lived, died and rose again are all evidence of this ultimate reality: the kingdom of God, the present reality of the rule of God. As we work to make simplicity a way of life in the midst of a culture that often tempts us toward duplicity, we have available to us a source of life quite invisible, but more real, more determinative, more reliable and more powerful than anything else we see. Yet we struggle to take hold of it.

■ When you think of the gospel, what typically comes to mind?

Jesus teachings

Jesus wanted his listeners to see and believe the invisible reality of his present kingdom. Read the following verses containing some of Jesus' words concerning the gospel.

Matthew 4:23: Jesus went throughout Galilee, teaching in their synagogues, proclaiming the good news of the kingdom, and healing every disease and sickness among the people.

Matthew 9:35: Jesus went through all the towns and villages, teaching in their synagogues, proclaiming the good news of the kingdom and healing every disease and sickness.

Mark 1:15: "The time has come," he said. "The kingdom of God has come near. Repent and believe the good news!"

Luke 4:43: But he said, "I must proclaim the good news of the kingdom of God to the other towns also, because that is why I was sent."

An illustration from the history of science reflects the significance of the invisible. In the mid-1800s, a disease known as childbed fever claimed the lives of an enormous number of women who delivered babies in hospitals. At its peak, as many as six of every ten women died in childbirth. During this same period of history, scientists in their laboratories began to wonder about the possible existence of invisible disease-transferring agents. The microscope had recently exposed a world invisible to the eye yet teeming with life, but the concept of contagion was still new. The early stages of germ theory had begun.

Some of those very same scientists also worked in the hospitals where women were dying at such alarming rates. And they noticed something—something we can barely imagine today: Doctors moved directly from the autopsy room into the delivery room without ever washing their hands.

Though this emerging germ theory had met with decades of skepticism prior to this, once accepted, the entire epidemic of childbed fever evaporated within a few short years. They had made only one small change: the doctors washed their hands.

Seeing the invisible reality matters. For women pregnant during the height of childbed fever, it made the difference between life and death. And for our own souls, seeing the reality of Jesus' kingdom can be a matter of life and death too.

Throughout our study we've highlighted just a few of the ways the world tempts us to live duplicitously; there are many others. For us to live consistently in simplicity, true to who God has made us to be, we need daily reminders of which kingdom we belong to: not the false, manipulative kingdom of this world, but the kingdom of God that is full of truth.

The various spiritual practices we've explored together over the past few weeks are what connect us intentionally with the invisible reality of God's presence—God's kingdom, God's purposes, God's love and grace and truth and power and, well, life. And they are what keep us connected, walking in his truth and living in simplicity for the long-term.

■ When do you most directly sense God's very real but invisible presence with you?

almost always now - I try to invite him in every day, to take over the helm -

■ When are you most likely to lose that awareness?

when external things happen that cause stress - I seem like I have to assimilate what is happening before I pray

84

When our souls are deeply rooted in God, as Dallas Willard explains it, we are the freest kinds of people—ones who can peer into the darkest needs of our day with confidence.

You've probably seen these bumper stickers: "Live simply so that others can simply live." I may not be too advanced, but somehow that never quite made sense to me. I just can't connect the dots between the number of sweaters in my closet and the starving masses in other parts of the world. And yet, I wonder, are we that connected? Are the dots really there, but I just can't perceive them?

The bumper sticker that does resonate with me is the admonition, "Think globally, act locally." What could that look like in real life? As it relates to our conversation about biblical simplicity and avoiding duplicity, those words remind me that I'm part of a much bigger community, the entire planet, and that my concern for the whole can find legitimate and meaningful expression right here. In essence, it urges me to act on the dots that I can see, even when my mind can't quite make the leap to global dots I can't see.

■ When you consider the "think globally, act locally" admonition, what comes to mind? Do what you can - Live intentionally

Here are some examples of how that takes expression in my life:

- Donation
- Recycling
- Relationships across racial divides

When I had a number of gently used baby things to give away (during a recent simplicity-oriented basement purging), I joined my local Freecycle group online. Within days, I connected with a family who had recently adopted two babies from Guatemala. The enormous expense of the adoptions (nearing six figures), plus the medical fees for the children, plus the general overload of adding new small lives to a household so quickly had prompted the mother of this family to join the Freecycle group, looking for help. She gratefully snagged some cute toddler hiking boots, a few jackets, some toys and several other items. And I loved knowing a new chapter of usefulness opened up.

In college, I majored in natural resources, which required courses in field biology, fisheries, forestry and wildlife, basic sciences, and resource management. Yes, I lined up with the tree-hugging, granola-crunching, rainforest-protecting types. I had little interest in becoming a forest ranger, but I was very interested in marine biology. (Scuba-dive and get paid for it!)

While that career didn't exactly materialize, I have always loved life and desired to protect and enhance it. Even now much of the work I do is to call people to a way of life—a sustainable way of life. Generally, that means intentionally connecting with God as the source of that life, teaching ways to intentionally care for the soul. But we live as embodied souls in a very real and physical world; the results of our physical way of life matter too.

Now, to be clear, I am not winning any awards from the Nature Conservancy. I have a recycling bin in my garage that is filled up every week (where does all that stuff come from?) and I drive a minivan with typical carbon emissions.

But I am growing in my awareness of the societal and global implications of my lifestyle. I am increasingly convinced that issues of social justice, poverty, environmental neglect and abuse, and racism are, in fact, rooted in the very market systems of which I'm generally a willing participant. I am learning more about this every day through books such as *Love God, Save the Planet* and *Justice in the Burbs.*

Again, we can't possibly adopt every issue that comes our way, but the universal call for each of us is to listen for that still small voice. How, if at all, is God inviting you to join in the many needs? Is there an invitation from him? We recycle - Care for animals - Educate people on reptiles. Try and live conservartly
■ Take time to pause, reflect, even ask God about that right now. Do you sense an invitation from him to learn more?

LORD, Share with me ways that you want me to do more than what I'm doing now -

5 GROUP DISCUSSION

Summary

Simplicity isn't a practice to be "done," like prayer or spiritual reading or fasting. Instead, pursuing a life marked by biblical simplicity becomes an overriding vision for one's entire life. In order to live in this vision, we need to see with more accurate eyes the world around us, and the world within us, and to move forward with great confidence into the future. Our peace is grounded not in pleasant circumstances—we all know life can be very confusing, painful and even bleak—but in the sure reality of God and his goodness, his presence and his ultimate victory over evil. Those grand ideas are best understood, seen and experienced in the gospel proclaimed as the kingdom of God—what Jesus shared as the good news. Perhaps a simplicity group will help you live out this vision. As you make progress toward simplicity in your life, the world around, both near and far, can and will be affected for good.

Opening

Describe a "simplicity moment" that happened to you since the group last met. What conversation, decision, purchase or corner of your life was recently influenced by what you're learning?

Discussion

1. What, if anything, did you sense God stirring in you through this fourth experience?

2. Go back over your written responses to parts one through four. What one or two ideas stand out as something you'd like to bring to the group? Why did they stand out to you?

3. Which spiritual practices have best helped you face truth—in an environment of grace—in the past?

4. Look up and read each of the four verses listed at the beginning of part three, including the entire passages in context. What practical meaning does the kingdom of God typically have for you?

5. What global concerns have captured your imagination or heart lately? How does the biblical concept of simplicity influence this issue, if at all?

6. Would your group transition well to the format of an AWOL group? What do you like about that kind of group, and what concerns or questions would that kind of group raise for you?

Prayer

Have one or several group members close this time in prayer, especially as this may be your final session! Pray for God to implant the strong idea of simplicity firmly in your life from now on, offering thanks for this "new thing" God has done (Isaiah 43:19).

"The life of every man is a diary in which
he means to write one story, and writes another,
and his humblest hour is when he compares
the volume as it is with what he vowed to make it."

J. M. BARRIE, AUTHOR OF *PETER PAN*

CONCLUSION

Confessions of a Naked Christmas Tree

Life is complex. It just is. As I finish this book, a few weeks overdue to the editor, I am sitting in my home office, surrounded by life: piles of books, CDs, partially completed projects and teaching notes. Farther out over the edge of my laptop, I see the Christmas stockings hung with care near the still-unopened boxes of (no, not gifts) Christmas ornaments! The naked tree stands slightly askew in the corner of the living room. At least it smells great!

I cancelled a meeting in order to finish writing (facing my limits), and yet had to drive my son's backpack all the way to his school, basically following him in his carpool (this is my life right now). Talk about waste! The basement is being refinished, so it's half-painted (read: half-unpainted) and the typical "store it in the basement" piles lurk in corners all around the house.

Oh, and the puppy used the doorframe as his chew-toy while I was gone this morning . . .

Sensing my frustration (this didn't require heroic levels of discernment), my husband gently kissed me goodbye as he left for the office, then looked back and said, "Remember to have fun!"

His words have stayed with me all morning; I sense God's quiet whisper within them. Jeff wasn't being trite or snide; rather, he sincerely called me back to what is most true. He knows I know it, and I know I know it.

All is well. All will be well. No matter what. Our limits are what they are. We run out of evening, and so the Christmas tree can wait. We forget our backpacks, and that's why I don't have a full-time job outside the home right now. We discover old resentments and have opportunity to forgive rather than fume.

I am also keenly aware that, at this very moment, other friends struggle with the tragic loss of their children, to death or coma. Some press on in painful marriages while others return to an empty house each night, hearing only the closing of the door behind them. And the suffering and injustice and destruction around the world continues, whether my Christmas shopping is done or not (which, as you might guess, it's not).

Does my little part matter at all? Does yours? Does my attitude right now, the "dot" in front of me, connect to the "dots" of my family, my community and the greater world around me? I believe they do.

Well, I am choosing simplicity. Embracing what is real . . . and finding freedom and joy. How about you? It's a bit like washing our hands—simple, maybe a bit obvious, but it changes everything, and brings life where there was death. The truest source of life is not anything or anyone other than Jesus. And his offer to me and to you remains: "I have come that they may have life, and have it to the full" (John 10:10). He is with me, right now, right here as I write. And he is with you, right now, right here as you read.

At Christmastime and every time, we can welcome the presence of Immanuel, God with us. It's not an easy life, but a real life. A with-God life. A life of single-minded devotion and trust.

A real, simple life.

Oh, and remember to have fun.

ALSO AVAILABLE IN SOUL CARE® RESOURCES

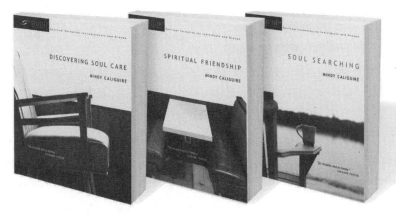

Discovering Soul Care	Spiritual Friendship	Soul Searching
978-0-8308-3509-6	978-0-8308-3510-2	978-0-8308-3521-8

To connect with Mindy Caliguire
and learn more about the SoulCare ministry
visit <www.soulcare.com>.